Twenty
NOVELISTS

Nigel Hunter

Illustrated by Edward Mortelmans

Twenty Names

Twenty Campaigners for Change
Twenty Explorers
Twenty Inventors
Twenty Names in Art
Twenty Names in Aviation
Twenty Names in Cinema
Twenty Names in Classical Music
Twenty Names in Crime
Twenty Names in Medicine
Twenty Names in Modern Literature
Twenty Names in Pop Music
Twenty Names in Sport
Twenty Novelists
Twenty Tyrants

Editor: Rosemary Ashley

First published in 1988 by
Wayland (Publishers) Limited,
61 Western Road, Hove,
East Sussex BN3 1JD, England

British Library Cataloguing in Publication Data
Hunter, Nigel
    Twenty novelists. – (Twenty names).
    1. Authors – Biography
    I. Title   II. Mortelmans, Edward
    III. Series
    808'.02'0922   PN451

    ISBN 1–85210–311–6

Phototypeset by Kalligraphics Ltd, Redhill, Surrey
Printed in Italy by G. Canale & C.S.p.A., Turin
Bound in Britain at The Bath Press, Avon

Contents

Novels and novelists

It is often said that a good novel is hard to put down. So, what is it that holds our attention in a novel? Partly of course, it is the story. The characters and events seize hold of our imagination. We want to know what happens next; we *care* – and sometimes we read on far into the night to find out. But the story is only one aspect of a novel.

Novels cover the whole range of human experience – whether comic or tragic, exceptional or everyday. Through their works, novelists provide us with insights into the lives and thoughts of characters who live in other times and places. They also help to give shape and meaning to our world.

No novelist can expect to please everyone, of course. Different people like to read different kinds of books. Some novelists who are popular for a while may later become quite unfashionable, and may even be forgotten altogether. Others continue to entertain new readers long after their own times are past. And others still – novelists who had faded into the footnotes of literary history – are re-discovered by later generations, who find new meaning in their work.

Knowing something about the writer can be helpful when it comes to appreciating their work. This book outlines the lives and achievements of twenty novelists of the past. Many of their names will be familiar; some, perhaps, less so. But they all wrote novels of lasting merit, which continue to speak to us today.

1

Miguel de Cervantes

Don Quixote by Miguel de Cervantes is one of the world's best-loved books. Even to those who have never read it, its two main characters are often quite familiar: the tall, thin, crazy old man of the title, and his short, dumpy companion, Sancho Panza. *Don Quixote* made fun of the medieval tradition of 'courtly romance' – and marked the beginnings of the novel, as we know it.

Cervantes led an adventurous life but one of poverty and misfortune. His family had fallen on hard times and his father made his living wandering around Spain as a barber-surgeon.

As a young man, Cervantes fought a duel in the grounds of the royal palace at Madrid. For this, he was sentenced to have his right hand cut off. He fled to Rome and became a soldier, fighting bravely and receiving serious wounds at the naval battle of Lepanto in 1571. Then he was captured by Moorish pirates and spent five years as

1547	born in Alacala in Spain
1569	writes first verses; flees Spain for Italy after a duel
1571	takes part in the Battle of Lepanto
1575–80	held prisoner by the Moors
1585	publishes *Galatea*, a pastoral romance
1588	commissions supplies for the Armada
1597	imprisoned for two months for irregularities in his accounts
1605	first part of *Don Quixote* published
1613	*Six Exemplary Novels*, a volume of stories published
1615	*Don Quixote* Part II published; also a volume of plays
1616	dies in Madrid

Right *The crazed Don tilts at windmills with his lance, believing them to be giants (a scene from vol. 1 of* Don Quixote*)*

a prisoner in Algiers. Finally, his family raised a ransom for him and he returned to Spain.

Cervantes' writing career began with a romantic novel and plays based on his years as a soldier. He also became a government agent, buying supplies for the Spanish Armada in 1588. Troubles with the government accounts led to imprisonment in 1597. In prison, however, he began to outline his masterpiece *Don Quixote.*

The book tells the story of a man obsessed by tales of medieval knights and their noble deeds. With his down-to-earth, simple-hearted squire Sancho Panza, the eccentric Don sets off on his horse Rosinante to do legendary deeds himself, seeing all the world as a stage for his exploits. Part One, published in 1605, brought them the fame they were seeking: in Part Two (1615) the two spend much time discussing it! The book's humour and wisdom brought Cervantes great renown in old age – and numerous appreciative readers ever since.

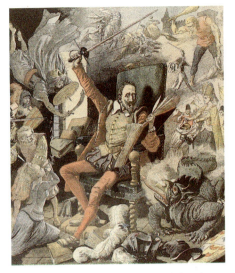

Above *Obsessed with tales of noble deeds Don Quixote dreams of future glory.*

2
Daniel Defoe

Daniel Defoe's novels were among the earliest in English fiction. *Robinson Crusoe, Moll Flanders* and *A Journal of the Plague Year* are probably his best-known works. Each book tells the story of an individual who manages to survive against the odds. The leading characters tell the story in their own words, and end by pointing the moral they have learned from their adventures.

Defoe's life was an extraordinary web of business, political intrigue and writing. All three activities landed him in gaol at various times. He wrote hundreds of articles, pamphlets and books, under a number of different names. Even 'Defoe' was partly invented. He was born plain Daniel Foe, the son of a London candle-seller, in 1660.

He became a merchant, dealing in many different commodities including hosiery, wine and tobacco. He was also involved in shipping insurance, and later, a brick and tile-making business.

Below *Defoe in the pillory: as a political satirist he outraged the government but was appreciated by many members of the public.*

But he never became prosperous: he first went bankrupt in 1692, and was often heavily in debt thereafter.

In 1685 Defoe took part in the Duke of Monmouth's rebellion against James II, and in 1688 he supported the 'Glorious Revolution' of William (III) and Mary, when they landed in England to take the throne from James. He was also beginning to write, producing pamphlets on political, economic and religious topics. For one satirical piece in 1703, he was put in the pillory – but instead of jeering, the crowd cheered him. To avoid further punishment he later became a government secret agent.

For several years he contributed to a political journal. He also wrote popular biographies of notorious criminals, to be sold at their executions. Defoe began writing novels only towards the end of his life. Despite their great popularity, however, they made him little money. He died in an attic while hiding from his creditors.

Above *'I was exceedingly surpriz'd with the Print of a Man's naked foot in the Shore'* – an illustration from the book Robinson Crusoe.

1660	born in London
1665	witnesses Great Plague, and Great Fire of London
1685	takes part in Duke of Monmouth's Rebellion
1688	joins forces of William of Orange (William III)
1703	gaoled for *The Shortest Way With Dissenters*
1704–13	edits the *Review*, a political journal
1719/20	*Robinson Crusoe; Captain Singleton*
1721	*Moll Flanders; A Journal of the Plague Year; Colonel Jacque*
1724	*Roxana; A Tour thro' the Whole Island of Great Britain*
1731	dies in London

3

Laurence Sterne

Laurence Sterne was born in Ireland, the son of an English army officer. He was educated in Yorkshire and at Cambridge University. He became a clergyman in 1738 and married three years later. His parish was situated close to York, where he often preached at the Cathedral. He was known for his eloquent sermons, some of which he later published, and for his political writings.

But he cut a strange figure for a clergyman – often visiting 'Crazy Castle', a friend's country house, where he found wine, bawdy conversation and a library of rare (sometimes obscene) books. Stimulated by these influences he began writing *The Life and Opinions of Tristram Shandy*.

The novel is an amazing medley of wit, farce, sentiment and learning. The narrative is full of startling twists and turns, digressions and jokes of every kind. One chapter is left out; two others are delayed; there are blank pages, black pages,

---

1713 born in Clonmel, southern Ireland
1733–7 studies at Jesus College, Cambridge
1759/60 publishers *The Life and Opinions of Tristram Shandy*, Vols 1 & 11; followed by *The Sermons of Mr Yorick*
1761/2 *Tristram Shandy*, Vols III–VI
1762–4 travels in France
1765 *Tristram Shandy*, Vols VII & VIII. Travels in France and Italy
1767 *Tristram Shandy*, Vol IX. Meets Elizabeth Draper, begins *Journal to Eliza*
1768 *A Sentimental Journey* published; dies in London

Right *On his way to deliver baby Tristram, Dr Slop is knocked off his horse by the family servant Obadiah – a scene from* Tristram Shandy.

'marbled' pages and diagrams. The book deals with such themes as birth, love and war; and with the links between thought, feeling and action. But it is chiefly concerned with time, and the processes of reading and writing.

Tristram Shandy, published in nine volumes between 1760 and 1767, gained recognition for Sterne throughout Europe. He was known as one of the wittiest and most original writers of the age. He became a celebrity and was invited to the most influential literary salons of London and Paris. He was considered a leader in the eighteenth-century cult of 'sentiment', or 'refined feeling'.

Sterne was now dying of tuberculosis but his illness seemed only to increase his appetite for life and humour. Under the name of 'Mr Yorick', he wrote two more books, *A Sentimental Journey* and *The Journal to Eliza*. His only real successors have been such twentieth-century writers as James Joyce and Samuel Beckett.

Above *An illustration from Sterne's book* A Sentimental Journey *featuring Parson Yorick, a character based on Sterne himself.*

4
Ann Radcliffe

Ann Radcliffe called her novels 'romances', and they were the best-sellers of the 1790s. Mainly describing the heroine's problems, with clear-cut heroes and villains and plenty of 'love interest' to sustain the plot, the novels bear certain resemblances to present-day 'romantic fiction'. But they were in fact the 'horror fiction' of their time: spine-chillers, with more than a hint of the supernatural; tales set in an imaginary Europe of wild, melancholy beauty and lurking terror.

Ann Radcliffe, born Ann Ward, spent her early life in London, the daughter of a tradesman. She grew up, however, in the fashionable city of Bath, with wealthy and well-connected relatives (her cousin was a doctor to George III). It is likely she attended a school run by two sisters, both novelists, named Harriet and Sophia Lee. At the age of twenty-three, she married William Radcliffe, a lawyer and journalist; and soon afterwards she began her writing career.

Right *Ann Radcliffe's fantastical, spine-chilling stories set amid wild, romantic backgrounds, tell of mysterious events. They are the forerunners of our modern horror-fiction.*

With her first two books – *The Castles of Athlin and Dunbayne* and *A Sicilian Romance* – she joined the ranks of the English 'Gothic' novelists. Their tales of dark intrigue and violent deeds (set in the past, and usually in foreign lands), had many enthusiastic readers, who eagerly seized on her next two books, *The Romance of the Forest* and *The Mysteries of Udolpho*.

The plots of her novels are concerned with virtue and vice in conflict: innocence and love threatened by evil, unrestrained passions. Gloomy castles, picturesque ruins and medieval monasteries provide many of her settings; wicked noblemen, evil monks, and brutish peasants are some of her villains. Scattered throughout the novels are poetic references and original verses, linking her work to that of other writers.

After travelling abroad for the first time, she wrote *The Italian*. This was as successful as her earlier novels but was the last book she published. She lived in retirement for the final twenty-six years of her life.

1764	born Ann Ward, in London
1787	marries William Radcliffe
1789	publishes *The Castles of Athlin and Dunbayne*
1790	*A Sicilian Romance*
1791	*The Romance of the Forest*
1794	*The Mysteries of Udolpho*
1797	*The Italian*
1815	Poetry from the novels reprinted as *The Poems of Mrs Ann Radcliffe*
1823	dies after long illness

5

Jane Austen

Jane Austen found the subject matter for her novels among the members of the small section of Regency society with which she was most familiar. Her stories are about the romantic attachments of young women, but her heroines are often faced with difficult choices before they finally settle for a comfortable and happy marriage. She viewed the world that she described with detachment and her writing is characterized by delicate irony and a fine sense of comedy.

Jane was born at Steventon, in Hampshire, England in 1775, into the family of a country clergyman. She was educated at home and she grew up with her sister Cassandra and six brothers in a quiet, happy, family environment. Reading aloud and play-acting were favourite family entertainments. In her earliest work, written purely for family amusement, she makes great fun of various fashionable styles of writing, such as the 'Gothic' fiction of Ann Radcliffe.

Right *A scene in Regency Bath, the fashionable city which features in many of Jane Austen's novels. She and her family lived there for several years.*

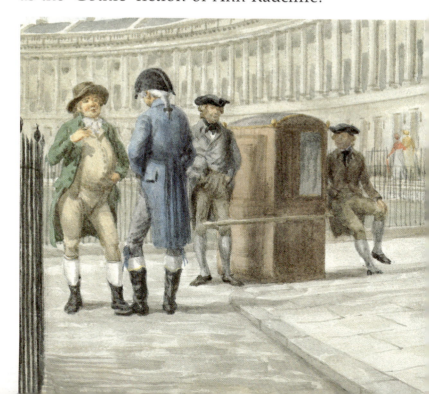

At about the age of twenty Jane began writing more seriously. She produced early versions of her first three novels but these were not published until considerably later. It seems she also experienced an unhappy love affair about this time. Then the family moved to Bath, with its famous spa-waters and wealthy social life. They lived there for four years, but Jane always preferred her quiet Hampshire village.

By her mid-thirties she was settled, with her mother and sister, in a small country house on land owned by her brother Edward. There, she revised two of her early novels. They were published in 1811 and 1813 as *Sense and Sensibility* and *Pride and Prejudice*. Three new novels, *Mansfield Park*, *Emma* and *Persuasion*, quickly followed. But *Persuasion*, along with the earlier *Northanger Abbey*, was published only after her death in 1817. Until then, her books had been signed simply 'By a Lady'. The unique appeal of their warmth, wit and subtle insight ensured their success with generations of readers to come.

1775 born at Steventon Parsonage, Hampshire
1787–93 writes earliest works including *Love and Friendship* and *Lady Susan*
1801–5 lives in Bath
1906–9 lives in Southampton, moves to Chawton
1811/13/14/15 *Sense and Sensibility; Pride and Prejudice; Mansfield Park; Emma*
1816 finishes last completed novel, *Persuasion*
1817 dies in Winchester
1818 *Persuasion* and *Northanger Abbey* published together

6
Alexandre Dumas

The Three Musketeers, The Count of Monte-Cristo, The Man in the Iron Mask – for these books and many others, Alexandre Dumas became the most popular writer in nineteenth-century France. He wrote colourful tales of swashbuckling adventure and intrigue, with romantic historical settings. To satisfy demand, he wrote at a furious pace.

Like many of his most dashing heroes, Dumas was a 'larger-than-life' character. His grandfather has been a French nobleman and his grandmother a beautiful Caribbean slave. Their son – Dumas' father – was a valiant general in Napoleon's army, but his widowed mother was not wealthy. Alexandre grew up in a small French country town; he received little education and at fourteen became a solicitor's clerk.

Then, attracted by the lure of the capital, Dumas went to Paris. He was employed in the office of the future King Louis Philippe. He also started writing sketches for the theatre. His play *Henry*

Below *A scene from the* Count of Monte Cristo *– the hero escapes from wrongful imprisonment and goes to the island of Monte Cristo, where he discovers a hoard of treasure hidden in a cave.*

III brought him fame, and later works like *Antony* and *Kean* established him as an influential forerunner of modern drama.

Both before and after his marriage to an actress he had many love affairs. His illegitimate son Alexandre (known as Dumas *fils*) later achieved renown as a writer himself.

Dumas began writing novels in the mid-1840s. His output was enormous – he wrote hundreds of volumes. Other writers often suggested the plots and he also employed people to punctuate and 'tidy up' his work. His books earned him great wealth, which he spent and gave away with careless abandon. He financed theatres and newspapers, and built himself a castle.

Dumas was a very popular figure and known as a great wit. He journeyed through Europe, North Africa and Russia. He was involved in various revolutionary upheavals, including the campaigns of his friend the Italian patriot Garibaldi, for the re-unification of Italy. Dumas belonged, said his countless admirers, to the world.

Above *A photograph of Alexandre Dumas, one of the great Romantic novelists of the nineteenth century.*

1802 born at Villers-Cotterêts, France
1823 employed by the Duc d'Orléans in Paris
1827–9 plays *Christine* and *Henri III* produced
1831–6 *Anthony* and *Kean* produced
1844/5/7 novels *The Three Musketeers, The Count of Monte-Cristo, Twenty Years After* and *The Man in the Iron Mask* published
1855 *The Mohicans of Paris*
1858 travels through Russia
1860–4 involved in Garibaldi's campaigns in Sicily
1870 dies at Puys, near Dieppe

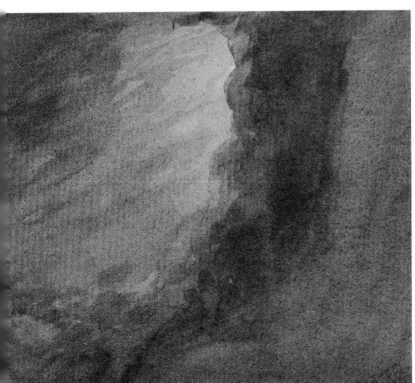

7
George Sand

'George Sand' was the pen-name of Amandine Aurore Lucile Dupin. She was, in her time, the most celebrated woman in Europe. Many of her novels reflected the circumstances of her life. They included works which revealed her own intense feelings and others that expressed her ideals of socialism. She wrote delightful tales about the countryside and long romantic novels. Early in her career she was notorious for her unconventional lifestyle, but her novels brought her prestige, and ultimately, respectability.

On her father's side, Amandine Dupin was related to the Polish royal family; on her mother's, to a humble bird-seller. She grew up in her aristocratic grandmother's country house in central France. In 1822 she married Casimir Dudevant, and the following year gave birth to a son. But she and her husband both had lovers and eventually, after the birth of their daughter, they agreed to separate and she went to live in Paris.

She lived at first with a young writer called Jules Sandeau. They wrote a novel together, and signed it 'J. Sand'. Thereafter, she wrote all her novels as George Sand. Her earlier novels, such as *Indiana, Valentine* and *Lelia*, were strongly personal, expressing her feelings about marriage and her feminist point of view. Her behaviour was considered scandalous – she had love-affairs with several well-known people, including the poet Alfred de Musset and the composer Frédéric Chopin, with whom she lived for nine years. She was famous among her contemporaries because she liked to wear men's clothing!

Her novels written in the 1840s, like *The Journeyman-Carpenter* and *Consuelo*, reflected her commitment to the workers' movements, beginning in France at the time. During the short-lived Revolution of 1848, she edited the *Bulletin de la Republique*. In later life she produced many more novels – also plays, essays, and numerous long, fascinating letters to friends. She died, internationally mourned, in 1876.

1804	Amandine Aurore Lucile Dupin born in Paris
1822	marries Casimir Dudevant
1831	lives with Jules Sandeau in Paris
1832	writes as 'George Sand': *Indiana* and *Valentine*
1833	Travels to Venice with poet Alfred de Musset
1834	first *Letters of a Traveller* published
1838	meets Frédéric Chopin
1840	*The Journeyman-Carpenter* published
1846	breaks with Chopin; *The Devil's Pool* published
1848	active in French Republican government
1850	begins relationship with Alexandre Manceau
1854–5	*Story of My Life*, vols I-XX
1857–65	*The Devil in the Fields; Confession of a Young Girl; Laura*
1876	dies at Nohant

Left *George Sand sometimes liked to dress in men's clothes, and in her younger days her unconventional lifestyle shocked many of her contemporaries.*

8
Nathaniel Hawthorne

Nathaniel Hawthorne wrote strange, sombre tales, 'romances' with many layers of meaning. They occupy a shadowy, mysterious area – 'neutral territory, somewhere between the real world and fairyland, where the Actual and Imaginary may meet . . .' In constructing his novels he drew deeply on his own sense of the past – especially the Puritan religious inheritance of New England.

He was born in Salem, Massachusetts in 1804, a descendent of one of the judges who presided at the infamous witch-trials there in the seventeenth century. His father, a sea-captain, died when he was just four. He was a quiet, solitary boy, happiest in the company of books and his own inward thoughts.

After leaving college in Maine in 1825, he shut himself away for twelve years in an attic room of his mother's old house in Salem, determined

Below *Before finding success Nathaniel Hawthorne spent twelve years in his mother's attic, developing his talents as a writer.*

to become a writer. He produced one novel, *Fanshawe*, which he later rejected as worthless, and a number of short stories which were collected and issued as *Twice-Told Tales* in 1837.

From 1839 he worked for two years as a customs official in Boston. He then lived for six months at Brook Farm; a socialist commune, and he later wrote about his experiences there in his novel *The Blithedale Romance*. Then, in 1850, after another period of work in the Boston Customs House, he published his first great novel, *The Scarlet Letter*. It is concerned with prejudice, passion and guilt in seventeenth century New England. The book brought him widespread recognition. *The House of the Seven Gables* and *The Blithedale Romance* quickly followed.

From 1853–7 Hawthorne was the United States consul in Liverpool, England; and afterwards he lived in Italy for two years. His last completed novel, *The Marble Faun*, was set in Rome. He died in New England in 1864.

Above *Nathaniel Hawthorne was one of the earliest internationally-renowned American writers.*

1804 born in Salem, Massachusetts, USA
1825–37 retires to attic room to write
1837 *Twice-Told Tales* published
1841 lives at Brook Farm community
1846 publishes collection of stories *Mosses From an Old Manse*
1850 *The Scarlet Letter*
1851 *The House of the Seven Gables; The Snow Image and Other Twice-Told Tales*
1852 *The Blithedale Romance*
1853–7 appointed American consul in Liverpool
1860 *The Marble Faun*
1864 dies in Plymouth, New Hampshire

9
Charles Dickens

Charles Dickens wrote all his novels for publication in magazines in serial form. His readers would discuss each episode excitedly as people discuss television dramas today. His stories teemed with unforgettable characters and exciting and emotional scenes. He dealt with a wide range of human behaviour and was concerned with many social issues – particularly the problems of city life, such as poverty and crime. Although Dickens wrote about Victorian England his work had an international, timeless appeal.

He was born in Portsmouth in England. Later the family moved to Kent and then to London. When his father went bankrupt in 1824, twelve-year-old Charles worked for some months pasting labels on bottles in a boot-blacking factory. He lived alone in dreary lodgings while the rest of the family had to stay in the debtors' prison. His childhood experiences in a frightening, hostile London deeply influenced his writing.

1812 born in Portsmouth
1824 works in bottle factory in London
1829–34 works as solicitor's clerk, court and parliamentary reporter; joins *Morning Chronicle*
1835–6 *Sketches by Boz*
1836–7 *Pickwick Papers*
1837–41 *Oliver Twist; Nicholas Nickleby; The Old Curiosity Shop; Barnaby Rudge*
1842 Visits USA; publishes *American Notes*
1843–4 *Martin Chuzzlewit;* first of *Christmas Books*
1846–50 *Dombey and Son; David Copperfield;*
1852–6 *Bleak House; Hard Times; Little Dorrit*
1858–9 reading tours; *A Tale of Two Cities*
1860–5 *Great Expectations; Our Mutual Friend*
1867–9 reading tour of USA
1870 dies, leaving *The Mystery of Edwin Drood* unfinished

When he was sixteen he worked as a clerk in a law office. Then he became a reporter. He began to write short, humorous sketches about London and his first sketch appeared in *Monthly Magazine* in 1835. In 1836 a collection was published as *Sketches by Boz*, with illustrations by George Cruikshank. Meanwhile his first novel, *The Posthumous Papers of the Pickwick Club*, was underway.

Other novels, including *Oliver Twist* and *Nicholas Nickleby*, soon followed and were widely acclaimed. He toured the United States and Europe. After publication of *David Copperfield*, much of it based on his own life, he established his own magazine. He continued writing and lectured on social issues as well as giving public readings from his work. He also enjoyed amateur acting.

The novels *Bleak House*, *Hard Times* and *Great Expectations* were among Dickens' greatest achievements. But his many activities took a heavy toll, and he died of a stroke in 1870.

Above *A Cruikshank illustration from Dickens'* Oliver Twist.

Below *Charles' experiences as a child worker influenced his writings and prompted a lifelong concern for social reform.*

10
Charlotte Brontë

Charlotte Brontë's novels are partly autobiographical and convey her strong personal feelings. She wrote about the problems of women in a man's world and about the possibility of finding love and spiritual fulfilment. Her heroines, plain and apparently uninteresting like Jane Eyre, survive lonely ordeals through courage and strength of character. Jane's story reveals what she felt at her 'heart's core'; and readers feel with her.

Charlotte Brontë was born in Yorkshire in 1816. She was the third daughter in a family of five daughters and one son. Shortly after the birth of her youngest sister Anne, the family moved to Haworth on the Yorkshire moors, where her father had been appointed rector.

After their mother's death in 1821, the four eldest girls, Elizabeth, Maria, Charlotte and Emily, were sent to boarding school where, within months, Elizabeth and Maria both died of tuberculosis. Charlotte and Emily returned home, to

1816 born near Bradford, England
1820 family moves to Howarth
1821 mother dies
1824 at Lowood School; elder sisters die
1835 teaches at Roehead
1839 becomes private governess
1842–3 studies with Emily, at Héger School in Brussels
1846 *Poems*, by Currer, Ellis and Acton Bell; writes *The Professor*
1847 *Jane Eyre* published
1848 Branwell dies Sept; Emily dies Dec
1849 *Shirley* published; Anne dies
1853 *Villette* published
1854 marries Rev. Nicholls, her father's curate
1855 dies
1857 *The Professor* published

24.-8.98.

18.9.98

1.10.98.

12.11.98.

19.11.98

grow up with their brother Branwell, and Anne, in extraordinary freedom. They came to know and love the wildness of the moors. They read many books together and created strange, imaginary worlds which they described in poetry and stories.

Later, Charlotte studied and taught at a school in Belgium, where she developed an unhappy attachment for the school's married director. In 1846, together with Emily and Anne, she published a collection of poems, under the pen-names of Currer, Ellis and Acton Bell.

Then each sister wrote a novel. *Jane Eyre* was published, along with Anne's *Agnes Grey* and Emily's *Wuthering Heights*, in 1847. Soon after, Branwell, who shared his family's literary gifts but was addicted to opium and alcohol, died of tuberculosis, and Emily and Anne also died, of the same dreaded illness.

After their deaths Charlotte revealed her sisters' true names. She published two more novels, *Villette* and *Shirley*. In 1854 she married a clergyman and died soon after, during pregnancy.

Above *The rectory and church at Haworth, on the Yorkshire moors.*

Below *An extraordinary family – Charlotte with her brother and sisters at Haworth Parsonage. Such happiness was all too short-lived.*

11
George Eliot

'George Eliot' was the pen-name of Mary Ann – or Marian – Evans. Her novels had serious moral themes, but they were written with liveliness and a gentle, subtle humour. Her writings reflect her belief that society is shaped by historical, political and personal forces. She wanted to widen the sympathies of her readers for their fellow humans, by showing how difficult individual circumstances could be. She hoped this would bring about a general improvement in the quality of life for everyone.

She was born in 1819 in Warwickshire, in the English midlands. She spent her early years on the estate managed by her father, and was sent to boarding school at the age of eight. Through the influence of one of her teachers and a local preacher, she became a convert to Evangelical Christianity. Later, however, she began to question the historical truth of the Bible. Nevertheless,

1819 born in Warwickshire, England
1850–3 works for *Westminster Review*
1854 meets George Henry Lewes
1857 *Scenes from Clerical Life* appears in *Blackwoods* magazine under 'George Eliot'
1859/60/61/63/66/72/76 *Adam Bede; The Mill on the Floss; Silas Marner; Romola; Felix Holt the Radical; Middlemarch; Daniel Deronda*
1878 death of George Lewes
1880 marries John Cross; dies after short illness

Right *Marian Evans (George Eliot) visiting a poor family on her father's estate. Her compassion for the plight of others was an important aspect of her novels.*

she remained strongly committed to many of its moral teachings.

After her father's death in 1849, she moved to London, becoming a full-time writer. She wrote articles about various subjects, and these appeared regularly in the *Westminster Review*, which she also helped to edit. In 1854 she met the writer George Lewes. He was married but lived apart from his wife, unable to obtain a divorce. They set up home together and their deep love for each other long outlasted the scandal of their relationship.

With Lewes's encouragement, she began to write fiction. Her first book, *Scenes from Clerical Life*, was widely praised. Many people wondered who 'George Eliot' was. The novels that followed, *Adam Bede*, *The Mill on the Floss* and *Silas Marner*, confirmed her as a writer of great merit. Her work reached its peak with *Middlemarch* and *Daniel Deronda*, vivid, captivating novels showing a keen insight into society and human nature.

Above *The range and depth of George Eliot's fiction has continued to captivate and entertain readers since the 1860s.*

13
Fyodor Dostoevsky

Dostoevsky created characters who held extreme attitudes and opinions – sometimes with states of mind bordering on insanity. They faced impossibly difficult dilemmas, clashing violently, and their author probed deeply into their minds. Although his novels are set in nineteenth-century Russia, they have prophetic qualities, recording the stirrings of bitterness and anxiety that were spreading in pre-revolutionary Russia.

Dostoevsky was born in Moscow in 1821. He was educated mainly at home, and later at a military school in St Petersburg. In 1839, two years after the death of his mother, his father, who was often ill-tempered and drunk, was murdered by the serfs who worked on the family's small country estate.

Dostoevsky's writing career began in 1846 with *Poor Folk*. This was highly praised, and he wrote three more short novels. He then became involved with a revolutionary political group, but

1821 born in Moscow
1839 enters military school in St Petersburg; father is murdered
1849 arrested as member of the 'Petrashevsky circle': reprieved on execution scaffold
1850–4 convict in Siberia
1854–9 serves as soldier in Siberia
1860 *Memoirs from the House of the Dead* published
1861 begins journal, *Time*
1862 visits western Europe;
1863 visits France and Italy
1864/66 *Notes from Underground; Crime and Punishment*
1868/71 *The Idiot; The Possessed (The Devils)*
1880 *The Brothers Karamazov*
1881 dies

they were soon arrested by the Tsar's police and sentenced to death. Seconds before execution, he and the others were told of their reprieve: the Tsar had wanted only to terrify them. Dostoevsky then spent four miserable years in a Siberian prison camp, followed by five years in the army. He married while in Siberia and returned to St Petersburg with his wife in 1859.

His account of prison life, *Memoirs from The House of the Dead*, was published in 1860. He edited two journals and travelled widely in western Europe. His unhappy marriage ended with his wife's death in 1863 and he married for a second time. His short, forceful novel, *Notes from Underground*, was published in 1864. He suffered from epilepsy and was greatly addicted to gambling, which put him deeply into debt.

Dostoevsky's later novels, including *Crime and Punishment* and *The Brothers Karamazov*, were his greatest achievements. They are compelling stories about the issues of morality, politics and religion, and are his lasting legacy to literature.

Below *Russian prisoners under guard in the wastelands of Siberia. Dostoevsky described his own similar experiences in his* Memoirs from the House of the Dead.

14
Leo Tolstoy

'A writer who lacks a clear, definite and fresh view of the universe . . . cannot produce a work of art,' wrote Count Leo Tolstoy. The characters in his epic novels undergo many disturbing, dramatic experiences. They are caught up in a sequence of events and are led to question their lives, their beliefs and the society in which they live.

Tolstoy was born into an aristocratic Russian family in 1828. His parents died when he was young and he and his brothers and sisters were brought up by their aunt and grandmother. They lived on a large country estate worked by serfs. His home education was followed by three years at university. For some time he led the carefree life of a wealthy young nobleman. Then he joined the army, fighting tribesmen in the Caucasus and taking part in the Crimean War of 1854–5.

Below *After emancipation Tolstoy attended to the welfare of his serfs, learning from their simple lifestyle.*

1828 born at Yasnaya Polyana, in Russia
1844–47 studies Law at University of Kazan
1851 joins army in the Caucasus
1852 publishes *Childhood*
1854 start of Crimean War; publishes *Boyhood*
1856 *Youth; Sevastopol Sketches*
1860–4 visits Britain and other European countries
1861 Russian serfs emancipated
1869/77 *War and Peace; Anna Karenina*
1882/86 *Confession* published (about his religious conversion)
1886 *The Death of Ivan Ilyich; Resurrection*
1904 *Hadji Murat* completed
1910 dies at Astapova railway station during flight from home

His earliest writings, based on these experiences, brought him fame, and praise from fellow-writers. But life in St Petersburg did not attract him and he travelled in Europe before settling down with his wife on his estate. Serfdom was about to be abolished and Tolstoy turned his attention towards the peasants on his estate, establishing schools and attending to the problems arising from their emancipation. He enjoyed the role of a progressive landlord and found that he learnt much from the peasants.

War and Peace, his epic novel of life in Russia at the time of Napoleon's invasion, was followed by the equally monumental *Anna Karenina*. Then Tolstoy's life changed dramatically. He became the leader of a religious cult dedicated to pacifism, poverty and a pure life, and his house became a centre of pilgrimage. His later novels and plays reflected his philosophy but his ideas caused bitter family rows. Eventually, aged eighty-two, Tolstoy fled his home, dying a few days later at the little railway station at Astapova.

Above *Towards the end of his life Tolstoy turned to a form of Christianity based on peaceful co-operation and a simple life-style. His home became a place of pilgrimage.*

15
Jules Verne

Jules Verne turned scientific discovery into an exciting world of fantasy. The thrilling adventures recounted in his books enthralled readers all over the world and later generations have been amazed by the accuracy of Verne's technological foresight. His books had also, like earlier forms of 'romance', a certain dream-like quality.

Verne grew up in the French port of Nantes in the 1830s. As a boy he tried to run off to sea but his father quickly caught up with the ship and young Jules promised that any future travels would be purely imaginary ones! Verne was expected to become a lawyer like his father, but his real interest was writing. His first play was performed in Paris in 1850. Thereafter, for several years, he was closely connected with the theatre. He also published a novel about love and revolution in South America.

Below *Captain Nemo inside his futuristic submarine* Nautilus, *astonished his captive – the narrator of* 20,000 Leagues Under the Sea.

He was unable to make much money as a playwright so he became a businessman, working on the stock-market. But he was becoming fascinated by new developments in science, and made lengthy notes on all the latest information. He married, and toured through Scotland and Scandinavia. Then in 1862 he resigned from business, saying that he had created a new kind of novel – and very possibly 'stumbled upon a gold-mine'.

Five Weeks in a Balloon was the first of sixty-two novels now recognizable as 'science fiction'. Such books as *Journey to the Centre of the Earth*, *20,000 Leagues Under the Sea* and *Around the World in Eighty Days* brought Verne wealth, honours and world-renown. He sailed his luxury steam-yacht around the coasts of Europe, and was fêted in every port. However, his last books expressed an increasingly unhopeful view for the future of humankind. He died just as the new 'atomic' age was dawning.

Above *An exciting moment for the explorers in* Journey to the Centre of the Earth.

1828	born in Nantes, France
1848	studies law in Paris
1852	novel, *Martin Paz* published
1862/64/65	*Five Weeks in a Balloon; Journey to the Centre of the Earth; From the Earth to the Moon*
1869	*20,000 Leagues Under the Sea*
1870	Awarded Legion of Honour
1973/75	*Around the World in Eighty Days; The Mysterious Island*
1888	Becomes town councillor in Amiens
1905	dies

16
Mark Twain

'Mark Twain' was originally a Mississippi boatman's call meaning that the water was two fathoms deep. It was an apt pen-name for Samuel Clemens for it recalled the happiest occupation of his life: but it also suggested two contrasting sides to his personality and his work. The humour for which he was famous concealed an increasingly bitter, hopeless vision of life.

Born in 1835, Sam grew up in the small town of Hannibal, beside the Mississippi River. There were six children in the family, and two household slaves. At the age of twelve, when his father died, Sam became an apprentice printer, and from 1853–7 he travelled round the country, working at his trade.

Then he visited New Orleans and became a river-boat pilot on the Mississippi, guiding the great paddle steamers with their colourful throngs of passengers up and downstream. Soon, however, the Civil War put an end to such times.

He became a soldier for a short time, then he went West, prospecting for gold. Eventually he became a journalist in California.

Before long Mark Twain's humorous articles were widely enjoyed. He was sent by his newspaper to the Pacific, to Europe and the Middle East. He returned to the United States to lecture and write about his trips. He married and settled in New England.

The setting for his great novels *Tom Sawyer, Huckleberry Finn and Pudd'nhead Wilson* was the river country of his childhood. Around the raft-ride of Huck and Jim, the escaped slave, he created a wonderful story of humour and social outrage – and a brilliant record of nineteenth-century America.

Twain was greatly honoured, but he suffered many sad losses in his personal life. At the end of his life he became a bitter and despairing man. One of his stories, written at this time and found locked away, suggested that life was just 'a grotesque and foolish dream'.

1835	born Samuel Langhorne Clemens in Missouri, USA
1840	family moves to Hannibal, Missouri
1857	becomes apprentice riverboat pilot
1861	outbreak of US Civil War
1864	joins San Francisco *Morning Call*
1865	story, 'The Celebrated Jumping Frog of Calaveras County'
1869/76	*Innocents Abroad; The Adventures of Tom Sawyer*
1878–79	travels in Europe
1882/83	*The Prince and the Pauper; Life on the Mississipppi* – memoirs
1885/89	*The Adventures of Huckleberry Finn; A Connecticut Yankee in King Arthur's Court*
1891–94	visits to Europe
1892/94	*The American Claimant; Pudd'nhead Wilson*; bankruptcy
1895–96	world lecture tour
1896–1909	deaths of two daughters and wife
1910	dies

Left *A scene from* The Adventures of Huckleberry Finn *– Tom, Huck and Indian Joe on their raft on the Mississippi, the river Mark Twain knew so well.*

37

17

Thomas Hardy

'The business of the poet and novelist,' wrote Thomas Hardy, 'is to show the sorriness underlying the grandest things, and the grandeur underlying the sorriest things.' The characters in Hardy's novels, set in nineteenth-century southern England in the region he called 'Wessex', live out their noble yet tragic lives in the countryside he knew so well. But the ancient traditions were beginning to change with the coming of the modern age.

Hardy was born and brought up in Dorset. His father was a master stonemason and his mother a domestic servant. He was educated at the village school and later in the nearby town of Dorchester. His mother encouraged him in his school work because she believed that education was the best way to overcome the formidable class barriers of Victorian England.

When he was sixteen, Hardy became an apprentice architect, working at the restoration

1840 born at Higher Bockhampton, England
1856–61 trainee architect
1862–7 architectural assistant in London
1871 first published novel, *Desperate Remedies*
1872 *Under the Greenwood Tree*
1873 *A Pair of Blue Eyes*
1874 marries Emma Gifford; *Far From the Madding Crowd*
1878 *The Return of the Native*
1886 *The Mayor of Casterbridge*
1887/91/95 *The Woodlanders; Tess of the D'Urbervilles; Jude the Obscure*
1898 *Wessex Poems:* first of ten volumes of verse
1902–8 writes *The Dynasts* (verse-drama)
1912 wife Emma dies
1914 marries Florence Dugdale
1928 dies

of country churches. Then he worked as an architect's assistant in London. He was writing poetry at this time but did not publish any of his verse until the end of the century.

Hardy began writing novels after returning to Dorchester, and he published the first of his 'Wessex' novels, *Under the Greenwood Tree*, in 1872. 'Wessex' became famed throughout the world through such novels as *Far From the Madding Crowd*, *The Return of the Native* and *The Mayor of Casterbridge*, and Hardy was welcomed by London literary society. But *Tess of the D'Urbervilles*, published in 1891, and *Jude the Obscure* (1895) flouted the moral and sexual conventions of the times and caused a public outcry. Hardy then returned to writing poetry.

He wrote an epic book about the Napoleonic Wars called *The Dynasts* which was greatly praised. He was unable to find happiness in his personal life but, by the time of his death Hardy was acknowledged everywhere as the 'Grand Old Man of English Letters'.

Above *Working in Dairyman Dick's yard – a happy interlude for the heroine of Hardy's tragic* Tess of the D'Urbervilles.

Below *Hardy's knowledge of rural Wessex traditions and his friendship with the local people gave his novels their unique character.*

18
Marcus Clarke

Marcus Clarke's *His Natural Life* tells the story of a cruelly twisted life – that of an innocent man sent as a convict to Australia. The gripping, powerful story, packed with exciting events and memorable characters, details the dreadful inhumanity of his punishment. The hero suffers terrible torments but his spirit is never quite broken. The main theme of the book is human evil, and the effects it has on individuals and on society.

Clarke was born in London in 1846. His father was a lawyer, his mother died when he was very young. While still a schoolboy, he enjoyed all the pleasures and vices of London's artistic society. He expected to inherit money when his father died in 1863, but in fact he inherited very little. So he decided to try his luck in the new colony of Australia, on the far side of the world. He had an uncle there who was a judge.

1846 born in London
1863 leaves England for Australia
1864 works in Bank of Australasia, Melbourne
1865–7 stays on cattle/sheep station, western Victoria; first writings printed in *Australian Magazine*
1867 becomes theatre critic of Melbourne *Argus*
1868 establishes the *Colonial Monthly;* novel *Long Odds*
1869 *Colonial Monthly* fails
1870 becomes official of Victoria Public Library; first instalment of *His Natural Life* appears
1874 novel revised – new title *For the Term of His Natural Life;* bankruptcy
1875–80 writes plays, pantomimes and stories
1881 second bankruptcy: dies

When Clarke arrived in the fast-growing city of Melbourne, his friendly outgoing personality won him many friends. His uncle found him a job in a bank but he was hopelessly unsuited to it. He went to live on a sheep and cattle station in the outback for two years. He spent most of this time writing, and entertaining the cattle hands with lively talks about French literature.

His writings about life in the outback brought him a career in journalism. He married an actress and began writing for the theatre in Sydney. He visited Tasmania, the large island south-east of Australia, where he saw the convict settlement with its grim old prison buildings. This prompted him to write his single great novel. It was published first in the *Australian Journal* in 1870; then, in altered form, as a book. After its publication, Clarke seemed only to waste his talent. Although apparently carefree, money troubles weighed heavily on him and he died in 1881 at the age of only thirty-five.

Below *During his period of penal servitude in Tasmania, Marcus Clarke's innocent hero Rufus Dawes is temporarily banished to solitary confinement on Grummett Island – only one of the terrible ordeals that befell him.*

19

Robert Louis Stevenson

Robert Louis Stevenson has always been a very popular author. With tales like *Treasure Island*, *Kidnapped* and *Doctor Jekyll and Mr Hyde*, he became an acknowledged master of story-telling. His most important works are concerned with the 'good' and 'evil' in human beings. Certain of his characters – for example Long John Silver in *Treasure Island*, and more obviously, Henry Jekyll in *Dr Jekyll and Mr Hyde*, – combine both good and evil in their personalities.

Stevenson was born in Edinburgh in 1850. He suffered ill-health all his life and his schooling was often interrupted. Stories told to him by his father and his nurse – romantic tales of adventure and of Scottish history – fed his imagination, and his nurse's religious views also had an important influence on him. The idea of 'Hell' terrified him – yet the thought of behaving 'sinfully' held a strong fascination.

1850 born in Edinburgh
1875–8 travels in France
1878 publishes travel-book, *An Island Voyage*
1879 *Travels with a Donkey in the Cevennes*; crosses Atlantic and USA to California
1880 marries; returns to Scotland
1881–2 *Treasure Island* appears in Journal *Young Folks*
1886 *Doctor Jekyll and Mr Hyde*; *Kidnapped*
1887 *The Black Arrow*
1888 cruises to South Pacific
1889 settles in Samoa; *The Master of Ballantrae*
1893 *Catriona*; *Island Nights' Entertainments*
1894 dies leaving masterpiece *Weir of Hermiston* unfinished

Right *Robert Louis Stevenson on the island of Samoa, where he wrote some of his finest works and where he is buried.*

His father, uncle and grandfather were famous engineers, and he was expected to follow them in an engineering career. He studied engineering, then law, at university, but rejected both careers in order to write. His family were upset by his decision and objected to his generally rebellious lifestyle, and there were many family quarrels.

In his twenties, Stevenson travelled in France, where he wrote *The Inland Voyage* and *Travels with a Donkey in the Cevennes*. There, he fell in love with an American, Fanny Osbourne, and followed her to California. They married in 1880.

He returned to Europe with Fanny and they lived first in Scotland and later on the continent. Stevenson wrote many of his greatest novels during this time although he was beginning to suffer severely from tuberculosis. In 1888–9 he made a tour of the South Seas and settled in Samoa with his wife and stepson. He died on the island and was buried with all the honours of an old-time chieftain.

Above *Stevenson's character from* Treasure Island, *the rascally pirate Long John Silver.*

20
Kate Chopin

For many years, Kate Chopin was almost completely forgotten. In her own time, she was known mainly as a writer of short stories. Nowadays she is admired most for her novel, *The Awakening*, the book which ended her career. The book describes the feelings and desires of a married woman. In 1899, it was considered shocking and sordid – today it is recognized as a feminist masterpiece.

Kate Chopin was born Katherine O'Flaherty in St Louis, Missouri, in 1851. Her mother came from a French-speaking Creole family, and French was Kate's first language. Her father died in a railway accident when she was four. As a young girl she enjoyed reading literature; she attended a convent school and grew up with her mother, grandmother and great-grandmother. All her life she had a great admiration for strong, independently-minded women.

Right *The final scene from Kate Chopin's* The Awakening, *which tells the story of a married woman's longings and desire for independence, in the days when such disclosures were considered scandalous.*

Kate married Oscar Chopin in 1870. During their European honeymoon – and afterwards – she enjoyed taking solitary walks, observing the life around her. Such freedom was quite unusual for a woman at that time.

They settled in New Orleans, where, before long she and Oscar had a family of six children. When poor cotton crops led to the collapse of Oscar's business, they moved to a village in Louisiana, where he opened a general store. Then in 1882, Oscar died. His widow continued the business for a while, then returned to St Louis to be with her mother – who also died soon afterwards.

Then began her tragically brief writing career. Her stories, set in the Bayou country of Louisiana, explored human relationships with great delicacy and insight, often concentrating on the experiences of women. But when her novel *The Awakening* was published, the public were appalled. She was devastated by the reaction to her book and published very little afterwards.

1851	born in St Louis, Missouri, USA
1855	father dies
1870	marries Oscar Chopin
1871–9	lives in New Orleans; birth of five sons and a daughter
1882	Oscar dies of swamp fever
1884	returns to St Louis
1885	mother dies
1889	first stories published
1890	novel, *At Fault*, published
1894	story collection, *Bayou Folk*
1897	second story collection, *A Night in Acadie*
1899	*The Awakening*
1904	dies from stroke at St Louis World Fair

Glossary

Autobiographical Of or concerned with one's own life.

Bawdy Humorous in an indecent way.

Creditor A person to whom money is owed.

Dilemma A problem that seems incapable of solution.

Emancipation Being set free from bondage.

Epic A long story involving many characters and events.

Epilepsy A nervous disease involving mental black-outs and fits.

Evangelical Christianity Religious faith based on the four Gospels of the New Testament.

Farce A humorous way of writing, involving absurd situations.

Fathom A unit of measurement indicating depth of water, equal to 1.83m (6 ft).

Feminist Someone who favours social equality for women.

Fiction A story involving imaginary characters and events.

Gothic A popular literary style of the late 18th century, characterized by 'horror' and the supernatural.

Irony A form of speech or writing which implies a meaning opposite to what is said.

Novel A long story, all or partly fictitious, dealing with character, action and thought.

Outback Australian bush country.

Pillory A wooden frame with holes for the head and hands, in which an offender was locked and submitted to ridicule.

Prophetic Having insight into the future.

Puritan A religious doctrine or attitude, involving strict moral laws or behaviour.

Regency In Britain, the period from 1811–20 during which the Prince of Wales acted as regent for his father, King George III.

Romance A story, novel, or long poem, often about events and characters that are remote from ordinary life.

Salon A meeting place, usually in a private house, where artists and writers could gather together socially.

Satirical Witty, ironic writing intended to show up the foolishness of an opposing point of view.

Serfdom The state of being a serf, bound to the land, especially in Russia before 1861.

Tsar The title of the Russian Emperor, before the revolution of 1917.

Tuberculosis A disease of the lungs.

Further reading

Austen, Jane *Pride and Prejudice* (Penguin, 1986); *Mansfield Park* (Penguin, 1986)

Brontë, Charlotte *Jane Eyre* (Penguin, 1986)

Defoe, Daniel *Robinson Crusoe* (Penguin, 1965; Puffin abridged, 1986)

Dickens, Charles *Oliver Twist* (Penguin, 1966; Armada abridged, 1980) *David Copperfield* (Penguin, 1987)

Dumas, Alexandre *The Three Musketeers* (Puffin, 1986) *The Count of Monte Cristo* (Puffin, 1986)

Eliot, George *The Mill on the Floss* (Penguin, 1986); *Silas Marner* (Penguin, 1987)

Hardy, Thomas *Tess of the D'Urbervilles* (Penguin, 1986)

Melville, Herman *Moby-Dick* (Penguin, 1984)

Stevenson, Robert Louis *Treasure Island* (Puffin, 1986); *Doctor Jekyll and Mr Hyde* (Puffin, 1985); *Kidnapped* (Puffin, 1987)

Twain, Mark *The Adventures of Tom Sawyer* (Puffin, 1985); *The Adventures of Huckleberry Finn* (Puffin, 1986)

Verne, Jules *Journey to the Centre of the Earth* (Puffin 1986); *Around the World in Eighty Days* (Scholastic Publishing, 1983) *20,000 Leagues Under the Sea* (Puffin, 1986)

Index

Picture acknowledgements

Ilustrations supplied by Mary Evans Picture Library pages 7, 9, 11, 21, 23, 25, 27, 29, 33, 35, 39, 43; Mansell Collection page 17.